Contents

Foreword	V
Introduction written by Joe's Grandson	VII
Granddad	IX
Old Beppo The Potter	XI
A Wrestler's Lament	1
Epitaph For Dead Lovers	2
The Ruined Paper Mill	2
Mad Hannah	4
A Kind Of Love	5
Despair	6
Buddhist	7
Poor Little Pig	8
Why?	8
A Coward Contemplates Suicide From Waterloo Bridge	9
Clouds	9
Campo Santo	10
Mars	12
Sunshine And A Litre Of Red Wine	12
The Unhappy Gardener	13
God's Office	14
Stones In A Millpond	15
Joy Ride	16
The Liddle Fad Boy	17
For Want Of A Better Word	18
Worms	18
River Bank	19
How I Would Have Said It	19
Come The Revolution	20
Death On A Level Crossing	20
Debut	21
The Dead Rat	21

I

The Olive Tree	22
The Widow	22
The Fool	23
The Fast	23
"T.V"	24
At The Bedside Of A Dying Man	24
Girls And Curls	25
You	25
Povero Zio Giorgio	26
Tell Them I Sleep	27
The Dancing Pig	28
The Eye	30
Prayer	30
Imprisoned	30
Invasion	31
A Change Of Heart	32
Lament To Lost Beauty	34
Death Of A New Born Babe	34
Hush Sweet Buttercup	35
Public Opinion	36
A Ready Woman	37
If I Had The Time	38
Reincarnation	39
Voices	40
Aftermath	41
36 Bus	42
Woman	44
The Little Boy Said	45
The Ugly Girl	45
Bliss	45
Amid The New Mown Hay	46
Dressing Room	46
Patterns In The Dust	47
Temptation	48

A Wrestler's Lament

And one hundred other poems

By
Joe D'Orazio

The Poet Laureate
Of
British Wrestling

Copyright © 2017 Joe D'Orazio

All rights reserved, including the right to reproduce this book, or portions thereof in any form. No part of this text may be reproduced, transmitted, downloaded, decompiled, reverse engineered, or stored, in any form or introduced into any information storage and retrieval system, in any form or by any means, whether electronic or mechanical without the express written permission of the author.

ISBN: 978-0-244-91474-5

PublishNation
www.publishnation.co.uk

Ode To A Nocturnal Creature	48
Graveside	49
Epitaph	49
Epitaph For A Globe-Trotting Wrestler	50
Can This Be Love?	50
The Addict	50
The Wedding	52
The Tramp	53
Sales Talk	54
Hypocrites	55
The Failure	56
The Price Of Friendship	56
Long, Long Ago	57
Too Late	58
The Four Ages Of Man	58
The Knell	59
Embakment Gardens	59
On The Roof	60
Funeral March	61
The Bell Of San Lorenzo	62
Death Of A Caesar, 1970	62
Winter	63
Resolution	63
The Man Who Never Would	64
The Prisoner	65
Another Day	65
The Strange Bird	66
The Sailor's Lament	66
Ad Infinitum	68
A L O N E	68
Fred	69
Sweet And Gentle Mistress Mine	69
Children Playing	70
When I Was Little	70

Income Tax	71
Space	72
Cupid	72
Tease	73
The Pleasure And The Profit	73
Promises	74
One Movement	74
E G O	75
To A Young Maiden	76
Sea Grave	76
The Lost Playmate	77
When I'm Not There	77
Why Pick On Me?	78
The Flame	79
In Conclusion	80
Me	81
The End	83

FOREWORD

Many people take the view
That those connected with
The wrestling profession
Are all brawn and no brains.
This book should help to
Dispel that belief.

I may not always have agreed
With Joe D'Orazio's
Decisions in the ring,
But as a modern poet I
Think he has great talent.

       Mick McManus

It wasn't all sweat blood & tears — a lot of it was fun
— Mick McManus

As written by Mick McManus in the 1990's.

INTRODUCTION

What follows in this book is a collection of poems written by my Grandfather. Many were written over 50 years ago, but they still maintain a good read today.

Born in Bermondsey on 27th July 1922 to Italian parents he was given the name Giuseppe Augusto Antonio Loreto Mario Scala. However he was more popularly known in the ring as Joe D'Orazio, and in promotional literature as Bob Scala.

Joe grew up in working class London and spent his early years working in his parent's fish and chip shop on the Old Kent Road. After the outbreak of the Second World War he became a member of a demolition squad clearing bombed buildings. Soon after he enlisted in the Royal Air Force and worked as part of The Air Sea Rescue for over 3 years.

After coming out of the RAF Joe decided to train in Judo and became a black belt in astounding time, taking just over one year. It was at this point that he also decided to follow his cousin Mike Marino and take up wrestling. His first professional bout was in 1948. In his time he has worked alongside many big names such as Mick McManus, Jackie Pallo, Steve Logan and many more. His time in the ring spanned twenty years, until he suffered a back injury in 1968 that made him decide to bring it to an end.

However Joe wasn't quite ready to throw in the towel. He continued to be a big name as a referee. He refereed at venues all over the country, amongst others, The Royal Albert Hall in London and Fairfield Halls in Croydon. For a further twenty years he travelled all around Europe to oversee some of the greatest names in wrestling.

What most people did not realise is that Joe was also very active behind the scenes. He worked for many years with Dale Martin Promotions and wrote hundreds of promotional articles with the name of 'Bob Scala', and took thousands of photos.

It was in 1971 that Joe released his first book which he wrote with Pam Edwards, 'The Who's Who of Wrestling' which was a hit from day one.

Outside of the world of wrestling Joe was very active. An artist in many forms, he loved photography, to read, write and paint and even became an actor and stunt man. He devoted half of his life working for Southwark Council, teaching adults with learning difficulties to paint, and continued working until the age of 93.

In the early 1990's after the disappearance of wrestling from British TV, Joe was still not ready to give up on his love for wrestling. He Co-founded The British Wrestlers Reunion which has become one of the largest reunions in the Wrestling World. Joe was made Life President in 2003.

At the time of writing this introduction, at the grand age of 95 Joe is one of the oldest living ex professional wrestlers and although isn't as nimble as he used to be, he is still able to make everybody in his presence laugh.

And finally taking inspiration from the man himself, I would like to end with a little poem of my own.

GRANDDAD

This man, he goes by many names
Giuseppe, Joe, Bob and Bobby

You may have seen him in the ring
But you didn't realise many a thing

He suffered bumps and bangs
And he even broke his nose
But when he got home
He would write his prose

Behind the scenes, he did the promotion
He would write the bill with utmost devotion

He brought new people into the game
And was the reason they shot to fame

This man, he goes by many names
Giuseppe, Joe, Bob and Bobby

I've looked up to him, since I was a lad
And I'll always call him, my Granddad

By Giancarlo Niccoli

OLD BEPPO THE POTTER

Before we begin with A Wrestlers Lament I have managed to sneak in a little story which has been borrowed from another of Joe's, as of yet unpublished books, entitled 'Old Beppo the Potter and Other Poems'. Whilst this story was not originally meant for this book, I felt it was too good to be missed.

A short time after the Second World War ended, I went to Italy for the first time and lived there for about a year on a farm a little south of Cassino.

During this time I made many friends... simple folk, farmers, railway workers, builders and their labourers, shopkeepers and the like. All of them honest direct men, all with some sort of philosophy to pass on, and such a man was old Beppo.

In Italy, if your name is Giuseppe... as mine is, they call you by your full name, or for short they may call you Peppino, Pepe, Peppo, Beppo, or any of another half dozen variations. Our little circle of friends used to call me Peppino... to distinguish me from another crony of ours... old Beppo.

Beppo was in his early sixties when I first met him, a giant of a man, he stood about 6'3" in his dusty sandals, and must have weighed about 23st. He had hands like two great bunches of bananas, and yet those same gigantic fingers were capable of turning out those pretty little earthenware pots that you can still find being sold on the market stalls all over Italy, for he was a potter by trade.

Beppo was the town hero, and it was rumoured that he had strangled more than 50 German soldiers during their occupation of the surrounding countryside. It's said that he use to creep about at night getting up to all sorts of funny things under the cover of darkness, but whenever I asked him to comment on the subject, he would answer by winking one eye, and at the same time tapping a huge forefinger against the side of his nose.

With his gravel voice and booming laugh, he was always the center of attraction, whether we were playing cards and drinking wine in the cantina down by the railway track, or merely passing the time of day in the middle of the piazza.

One night, old Beppo didn't turn up for a promised Saturday night game of cards, and after cursing him for spoiling our plans, we split up and found ourselves other things to do.

Next morning I was walking up the long dusty road that led from the farm to the town, when Beppo's eldest son Vittorio came running after me. "Come quickly Peppino" he said, "My father wants to see you… he is dying."

Beppo's wife Maria was saying the Rosary at the top of the stairs when we arrived, and she ushered us into the bedroom without missing a single Hail Mary. I found Beppo's enormous frame propped up in bed by the aid of about three dozen snowy white pillows. Of course he was dying… it was written all over him.

"Beppo! You cunning old bastard" I said, waving a fist at him. "What are you doing?"

He smiled weakly.

"What am I doing Peppino?... I'm dying."

I swallowed hard.

"You can't die, you cunning old fox, you still owe us all money. We need you for the card game on Saturdays."

He spread his great big fingers out wide on the counterpane in a helpless gesture, then beckoned me to come closer.

"Peppino, will you do one little thing for me when I am gone?"

I couldn't answer.

"Will you write one of your little poems for me? Just a little one about Old Beppo the Potter, so that my friends will not forget me?"

We buried Beppo a couple of days later... they don't leave you lying about very long when you die in Italy. After I came back down the hill from Campo Santo, I wandered into Beppo's yard. Over in the corner of the yard was a lean-to shelter where Beppo used to work out of the glare of the sun. In the corner of the lean-to was his potter's wheel.

I put my foot on the treadle and worked it the way I had seen him do a thousand times... "Ker-lonkitty, clonkitty, clonk" it said... "Kerlonkitty, clonkitty clonk."

What was it the wheel was trying to say to me?... I tried again.

"Ker-lonkitty, clonkitty, clonk"...
"Old Beppo the Potter is dead"... It was coming through.
I could understand every word it was saying. It was telling me the words for Old Beppo's poem... I scribbled them down on a piece of paper.

Old Beppo the Potter is dead
Old Beppo the Potter is dead
No more will his wheel
Respond to his heel
In time to his nodding head.

We've taken him up
To the Campo Santo,
That stands at the top of the hill,
And buried his body to make more clay
For his sons to use on his wheel.

And should my children pass this way,
They'll buy those pots I pray
For 'though they may find better pots,
They'll not find better clay.

XIII

XV

A WRESTLER'S LAMENT

I'm just about fed-up with this game
With its bumps and its bruises and bangs,
And the dear sweet old ladies of ringside
Sharpening their claws and fangs.

The soft fat man with his blonde girlfriend,
Who jabs with lighted cigar butt.
The bald-headed vulture, whose battle cry
Is, "why don't you get your hair cut?"

Those wicked old mums with hatpins
Ready to maim and kill.
Umbrellas at the ready,
Wielding stiletto heel.

Types our dear forefathers
Would have burned at the stake.
Pencil necked youths with long lank hair
Who greet every fall, with "Fake"

The jeering shouting ignorant lot
Smelling of smoke and rain.
I wish they'd jump in the river
Then I could pull the chain.

The Din: The Clamour: The peanut shells:
The microphone booming above it.
I'd leave it tomorrow, I would, I would
But the trouble is… I love it!

EPITAPH FOR DEAD LOVERS

Embrace us to thy breast dear Mother Earth
That we might share with none,
The solitude, that in our lives
We shared with everyone.

THE RUINED PAPER MILL

Along the white and dusty road
Over the sleepy hill,
Down by the River Liri's edge
Stands a ruined mill.

Here it was in bygone days
They brought the trees they fed
With strong brown hands into machines
To earn their daily bread.

Here too, with mighty iron teeth
The wood was ripped to shreds,
And pulped and soaked and pressed and dried
And stored in airy sheds.

But now all this is past
And overgrown with weeds
Yet still she stands on guard
A Cenotaph to former deeds.

So, still the Liri bubbles past,
Shooting her spray, like oxyacetylene sparks,
High into the azure sky
To land among the meadowlarks.

And, where once I leaped
Bare footed o'er the rocks
I lay well satisfied to watch
The distant shepherd tend his flocks.

For now I'm fat and heavy
And slip and slide,
With no small loss of dignity
Where once I walked with pride.

Wishing my spine, strong roots would show,
And searching deep their fingers run.
That from my loins a tree would grow
To shade me from the mid-day sun.

MAD HANNAH

Near thirty years since and yet,
Still Mad Hannah walks the streets
Weeping for her slaughtered love.
The love she saw decapitated die
On the blood soaked pavement
Of the crimson city.

Now all is pain and sorrow.
And as she darts
To screech at lovers passing arm in arm.
Her burning brain remembers
Only his headless body and the never ending pain
That began with the birth of their stillborn child.

The urchins
Call her names
And run away.
And, to their eternal shame
The grown-ups smile,
As if they are superior beings.

But I remember Hannah as she was
In those last few days before the bombs came.
Swollen with child, and the bloom on her like a ready peach.
With the light of love
Shining from the soft brown eyes
That could see only him.

How she roamed the streets like a Roman cat,
For seven nights whilst the city burned.
Searching for her faceless love,
Calling his name and cursing God and all men,
Still carrying within her
The child of his already withering loins.

Pity, pity, poor Mad Hannah,
But pity even more,
Those who cannot pity her
And turn her from their door.

A KIND OF LOVE

There is a kind of love
That far transcends
The feeding of an appetite
Or seeking justification for being more than friends.

Or the holding of hands
Or catching of eye,
Or the touching of fingertips
Or the sharing of a sigh.

There is a kind of love
That lends itself to everyday,
In which, distance matters not,
For we are but a thought away.

And in which the passing of time
Matters to no degree.
There is a kind of love,
And such I have for thee.

DESPAIR

Despair, despair, dull despair.
I rack my brains and tear my hair.
But all in vain, to no avail
They still pour in by every mail.

Dear Sir, we very much regret unless …
Telephone, Rates, O.H.M.S.
Gas, Electric, School Fees too,
What on earth am I to do?

Surrounded by foes on every side
In desperation try to hide.
Perhaps I could pretend I'm dead,
But who would earn our daily bread?

Butcher, Baker, Milkman too,
Gather outside and form a queue.
Ring my bell, then wait with smirk
Know I haven't gone to work.

Go to see the Parish Priest,
Know he'll try to help at least.
"Come in dear boy, how long has it been?"
"Like to help, but haven't a bean".

"Need more money for the church,
Government's left us in the lurch"
"There's a box just near the door
Leave some pennies for the poor"

The POOR? That's me, why can't he see?
Is there nowhere left to flee?
Going down on bended knee.
"Lord, O Lord, O PLEASE help me"

BUDDHIST

Tread softly, so as not to wake
The vines that gently climb.
For fear they lose the harvest
And yield us not the wine.

And always walk with dignity
When passing willow tree,
Last thou offend its noble cause
Or spoil its symmetry.

Think well on each foregoing step
And place thy feet with care,
Lest in a moment of ill haste
Thou crush the insects there.

POOR LITTLE PIG

The little pig looked up at the stars
That shone in a black velvet sky,
And quite overcome with emotion
The little pig started to cry.

"How cruel of God to create me thus,
He couldn't have cared a fig.
To put the soul of an artist and poet
"Inside the skin of a pig"

"It's not as if I'd have asked for much
Just a garret, some paints and a brush,
The sweet silver notes of the meadow lark
And the cheerful song of the thrush"

"Instead it's my fate to end up on a plate
Alongside of fried eggs and chips.
And I'll see no more of this lovely world
As I pass through some glutton's lips"

The little pig looked up at the stars
That shone in a black velvet sky,
And quite overcome with emotion
The little pig started to cry.

Then God in his mercy, felt sorry
So he sent down the sun, wind and rain.
To dry up the tears, and blow away fears,
And wash away some of the pain.

WHY?

"Why was Jesus white?"
I once heard a black child say.
I couldn't answer her then,
Any more than I can today.

A COWARD CONTEMPLATES SUICIDE FROM WATERLOO BRIDGE

How cold the distant water seems
And yet the deed must now be done.
A little step will end my dreams
And I will never see the morning sun.

For life has been and passed me by
I've never had a chance.
The time has come for me to die,
And still you pass without a glance.

See…now I mount the parapet
Which proves I mean to do the deed.
And who is there to mourn? I ask,
Or help me in my hour of need?

Not one of you has looked my way
As home you hurry to your beds.
Not one of you, my hand will stay,
Then let my blood be on your heads.

Forgive me Lord, my final sin.
Farewell O World, I here give up the fight.
DEATH? I leap to meet thee with a grin.
Look! I jump. I jump… BUT NOT TONIGHT.

CLOUDS

How clever of God to make a cloud,
How clever of God, he must have felt proud.
When he puffed out that little white cotton wool ball,
He must have been thinking of us all.

But there's one thing I hope he'll excuse me for saying,
If not…I'll make up for it next time I'm praying,
Although we would be in a state without any,
I do wish he hadn't made quite so many.

CAMPO SANTO

Through the iron gates
Where once my Nonno turned the key,
There stands the peaceful place
They call the Cemetery.

And here at final rest
Sleeping ever in the sun,
Lay both rich and poor alike,
Whose days on earth are done.

And the troubles that beset them
In this our mortal life,
Have been buried with them
And no longer cause them strife.

And here it matters not
The cut of cloth or shape of shoe.
Or whether 'tis best to wear,
The yellow, red or blue.

For dressed alike
In coat of common clay,
They wait in patient file
Upon the Judgement day.

Such happy solitude as this
Would be most difficult to find.
On every hand a graven name
Stirs some dark corner of the mind.

Was this the man who once I met
At the christening of someone else's son?
Was this the girl I can't forget
Who lays here sleeping in the sun?

Was this the man who ground the corn
A hundred years 'fore I was born?
Who died at the age of thirty-one,
And this…his eighty-year-old son?

How will they greet
When next they meet?
This wrinkled old man whose picture I see,
Will he sit on his young father's knee?

This raven haired beauty with soft and placid smile,
For whose death, her husband did stand trial.
What grand tragedy of love and hate.
Enough to last one all one's days,
And fill the minutes of a year.

And on this pretty plot
Of marble, dust and clay,
One could keep well occupied
For every living hour of the day.

And in the evening
When the sun goes down aglow,
Retrace our earlier footsteps
To the sleepy town below.

And from our watching windows
Gazing ever up the hill,
See the stately Cypress trees
Stand silent sentinel.

MARS

I am the greedy God of war
Who comes with bomb
To plough the green, green fields
And seminate the hungry furrows
With the bodies of the stinking dead,
That they might fertilise the land
And grow me battlefields afresh.

SUNSHINE AND A LITRE OF RED WINE

That's all I need,
Some sunshine and a litre of red wine.

A piece of bread perhaps,
Un pezzo di formaggio, and maybe a big onion.

What more could a man ask for
Beneath an Olive tree surrounded by old friends?

I've seen the Inglesi
When they drink our wine, pull faces and shudder,
If they don't like our wine,
They should drink milk straight from the cow's udder.

THE UNHAPPY GARDENER

Would'st that I could pluck a rose
And graft its petals on thy cheeks,
That they might hide
The wrinkles etched by time.

Or gather dew-drops by the score
To bathe the sparkle back once more
Into thine eyes,
And wash away thy tears.

But life is not a garden, nor have I the power,
So, when thy beauty fades, as fade it must,
I shall love thee then for what thou ar't
Until we both are turned to dust.

GOD'S OFFICE

God sat in his big shiny office
Puffing a big cigar.
He'd just had words with Saint Peter
Who he had sent out to hose down his car.

"I ain't an unreasonable guy" said God
To his typist Miss Magdalein,
"And I don't like throwing my weight about,
But I have to, now and again".

"Take Pete for instance, I've know him for years,
And I've always treated him well,
But when I asked him to wash down the car
He told me to go to Hell"

"I know his feet are playing him up
And he's old and running to fat,
But after all, I am God,
He can't talk to me like that"

"I don't like to pension him off, you see
After working so long on the door,
But trade ain't as good as it used to be
If it keeps up, we'll all be poor"

"So have a word with him on the quiet
And tell him the way things stand.
Say I'm confident we'll pull through
If only he'll give us a hand"

"Explain that at least it's better here
Than to burn in eternal Hell fires.
And tell him that while he's about it, the bum,
To put some more air in my tyres".

STONES IN A MILLPOND

When did I last reach out
And touch a star?
Or throw stones at the moon
In a mill-pond?
Or make love with Mother Earth
As I stretched out on my belly
To suck the ice cold water
From the fierce flowing streams
Of the Abruzzi?

When did I last hear the howling of the wolf
Up on the mountain-side in winter?
Or listen to the wisdom
Of an old man's philosophy?
Or, with a litre of red wine
And a piece of cheese,
Spend a whole day dreaming
Under the shade of a friendly walnut tree
In summer?

When did I last set free my mind
And let it soar
To the inaccessible places?
Or feel the rhythm of a kindred heartbeat
Next to mine?
Or swim in terror
Across the bottomless lake
Into the aching limbo land
Of unrequited love?

JOY RIDE

"Now it's obvious" says the professor
"That this 'ere bloke is dead.
An' to judge by the bleeding great 'ole in 'is bonce,
I would say 'e's been 'it on the 'ead

" 'Owever don't let us be 'asty
We don't want to make no faux pas.
You take 'is arms, an' I'll take 'is feet
An' we'll stow 'im in back of the car"

Much easier said than done, I'm afraid
On account of him being so tall.
So we laid him out on the roof rack
And made for our first port of call.

We called at "The Magnet", "The White Horse Inn".
"Princess Alice", and "William Tell".
And it must have been nearly 10.30p.m.
When they slung us out of "The Bell"

We had to drive past the coffee stall
That stands just over the bridge.
The professor had a pie with sauce,
And I had some eels from the fridge.

It was half past eleven when we got home
And drew up two chairs by the fire.
We'd brought in the corpse on account of the rain
As inside, we thought he'd keep drier.

"Poor old chap" the professor said
" 'e aint a day over forty.
We should have taken him to the police
Let's face it, we've been rather naughty"

"A little drop of the hard stuff
Will cheer us up no doubt"
And he went across to the sideboard
And brought a bottle out.

He poured out the amber liquid
Smacking his lips with glee.
At the stroke of twelve, the corpse sat up,
And said, "What about one for me"

THE LIDDLE FAD BOY

Oi be a liddle fad boy
Oi be.
A liddle fad boy
Oi be, oi be.
Oi be a liddle fad boy
Oi be.
A liddle fad boy
Oi be.

FOR WANT OF A BETTER WORD

A tenderness of thought.
A tenderness of speech.
A tenderness of touch.
One thing leading to another.
For want of a better word,
They call it ... Love!

An intermingling
Of unspoken thoughts.
A rhythm of words.
A warmth of contact.
For want of a better word,
They call it ...Love!

A co-ordination of movement.
Of soft undulating curves and deep crevices.
An economy of rhythm, abandoned to spasmodic un-rhythm.
A flooding of my mind, with your most secret thoughts.
There is no better word,
Let's call it ... Love!

WORMS

Such short interlude we spend,
Above the musty ground.
Whereon we dance, and pose and prance
And make with boisterous sound.

But all too soon, victorious worms,
Will stand in file, and take their turns
To wriggle with convulsive glee,
And dance their merry jigs in me.

RIVER BANK

All along the river bank…
Willows weeping, hedgehogs sleeping,
Come the soft, soft sound of ripples,
Gently rippling, softly trickling.
Flap, flap, flap, upon the water,
Fat ducks scurry,
In a hurry.

All along the river bank…
Toads are croaking,
Bees are stroking
Pollen from the clover beds.
Hedgerows shimmer, bluebells glimmer
As they nod
Their jangling heads.

All along the river bank …
Lovers walking, softly talking,
Heads together, eyes adoring,
Silk soft fingertips exploring.
Lost in love's ecstatic quiver
See not the moon
Caress the river.

HOW I WOULD HAVE SAID IT
(If I had been Cardinal Wolsely)

What a berk I was
To have served my King
Instead of serving my God.
For HE wouldn't have left me
All alone,
To die like a poor old sod.

Of Cardinal Wolsely it has been said…
"He was born in Ipswich,
And died in bed".

COME THE REVOLUTION

When the revolution of the mind
Comes at last to overthrow the old regime
That makes us sorrowful and sad,
Then those who think in other vein
Will judge, and of necessity
Pronounce us mad.

And when they lock us up
Within our little rooms,
That we may gaze upon the sky though iron bars,
In our silent solitude
We'll read and write,
And in the cool of evening, look upon the stars.

DEATH ON A LEVEL CROSSING

How undignified!
Laying in the road
With her legs apart.
Blood everywhere.
Most undignified.
How undignified!
On a Zebra crossing too,
There's the irony of it.
Bad enough in bed, but on a zebra crossing!
How undignified.

How undignified!
Audience jostling for better view.
Standing room only. The final curtain.
No repeat performance. No matinee tomorrow.
…So undignified.

DEBUT

When I was born
They held me upside down
And smacked my arse,
That I might weep
For all the World.
For all the World
And all it's woe's
At least, that's how
The story goes.

But having been around some time
That's not the way my thoughts incline.
In fact it's very plain to see
The one I wept for then was me.

THE DEAD RAT

I saw a dead rat
Killed by a savage cat.
Now mummy rat
And baby rat,
Wait at home
For daddy rat.

THE OLIVE TREE

It's a miracle, to one like me,
That such a gnarled and twisted tree,
With Mother Earth can work and toil,
And channel unto us, her oil.

For was there ever richer gain
From oceans deep, or fields of grain,
As this derived from rocky grounds
That in this sun scorched land abounds?

And what could ever man construct,
That could replace this olio duct?
For no machine however bold,
Could promise us, this liquid gold.

And just as for a million years,
And for a million years to come,
So should we all be well content
And satisfied with what God's done.

THE WIDOW

A widow,
She wears her weeds well.
Seeking not
The company of men
Nor yet avoiding it.

Taking each day as it comes
As if to say "Life must go on"
As indeed it must.
For he would have wanted it this way.
He who is turned to dust.

THE FOOL

How cruel is life, how cruel, how cruel,
To those of us who play the fool.
And yet, as if to make amends
She showers us with many friends.

And so, when all is said and done,
Perhaps I am the lucky one.
For wiser men than me there are
But I'm the happier one, by far.

THE FAST

The bell that rung our love
Has lost its tongue.
As we who lose our youth
Remain no longer young.

However this fact indeed remains,
That we at least have shed our chains.
And freed from appetite at last,
With dignity we keep the fast.

"T.V"

Such fantasies of light
That strike upon
The very mirrors of the mind
And with probing fingers
Cold as ice
Benumb our very brain,
Will in time
Consume us all.

Then hail the new generation
When, by surgeon's knife,
And a small incision,
A discreetly placed computerised cell
Will herald the birth
Of a brave new era,
And send us marching
To our brave new Hell.

AT THE BEDSIDE OF A DYING MAN

What say you then old man,
That all is done when last we close our eyes?
Come answer whilst the spark of life I fan
To flame again, one last moment' ere it dies.

For this you swore, that as you left the realm of man,
You would to me, with dying breath impart
The secret, which since our world began,
Has ever taxed and worried mankind's heart.

See, now his lips begin to move, now shall I learn
He beckons with his eyes and lifts his aged head.
"Yes, yes" I cry, and in reply,
He sighs, and falls back… dead.

GIRLS AND CURLS

Why can't
Pretty little white girls,
Have pretty little tight curls
Like pretty little black girls.

YOU

There is no scar so deep
I cannot heal with love.
No mark, or sign of injury
I cannot kiss away
And make as new again with love.

For any sign of imperfection, however small,
Serves but to make you... you.
Take them away and you would be,
As all the others…
And no further use to me.

The scars upon your mind then
I shall kiss away.
The others? … Let them be.
For they are but the silver chains,
That bind you close to me.

POVERO ZIO GIORGIO

Poor uncle Giorgio
With snow white hair
Sitting there in the sun bleached chair
Wrapped against the evening chill
Watching the sun set on the hill.
Poor uncle Giorgio.

Poor uncle Giorgio
Watching the cockerel in the dust
Peck at the fallen grapes
Like the instrument of some inquisitor
Pecking at the eyes of a tortured world.
Poor uncle Giorgio.

Poor uncle Giorgio
You've seen it all
The wars, the peace
And all the terrible and beautiful
Times in between.
Poor uncle Giorgio.

Poor uncle Giorgio
You've not the strength or will
To eat, or sip the wine
That would give you strength
To eat and sip again.
Poor uncle Giorgio.

Poor uncle Giorgio
Nor can you hear the pipes
Of the shepherd boy upon the hill
As he calls his flock together
For the night.
Poor uncle Giorgio

Poor uncle Giorgio
The sun has washed the colour
From your eyes
And made the hardness soft
Like the eyes of angels.
Poor uncle Giorgio.

Poor uncle Giorgio
There isn't one that doesn't love you
Or feel a certain tenderness in your presence,
What a rich, rich,
Rich, rich man you are.
... Poor uncle Giorgio.

TELL THEM I SLEEP

Tell them I sleep
In a marble bed
With cypress'
Towering overhead.
'Neath blanket of green
I dream my dream,
The present, the future,
And what has been.

And should they ask
As to my life,
Say I left behind a wife
Who to herself
And me was true,
And never gave me
Cause to rue.

But, with soft
And warm caress,
Filled all my nights
With tenderness.

THE DANCING PIG

I once met a pig that was dancing a jig
Right at the top of a hill
And for all that I've heard to the contrary
He is probably dancing there still.

Came his mother that day, and said "Pig I pray,
I have baked you a Trimbledew Pie,
So please will you stop, spinning there like a top,
Table is laid in the sty"

Said piggy, "I fear I must remain here,
I have promised my sweetheart I would"
"And If I should stray, and she passed by this way,
She would certainly leave me for good"

Then his mother spied me, and said "Sir, follow me,
Have you not tasted Trimbledew Pie?"
I answered "Oh yes" Though to you I'll confess
That I hadn't, but fancied to try.

So we sat down to dine, and she brought out the wine
Which we drank from two goblets of gold.
The pie was delicious and when we were finished,
This is the story she told.

"Poor pig has quite fallen in love sir" said she,
"And the matter has caused me much pain"
"He has gone off his food and to make matters worse,
Stands dancing the jig in the rain."

"Many times have I prayed and such plans have I made
For the day that young pig should wed"
"Now he's fallen so badly, so utterly madly,
For a dancer with tresses of red"

"She passed by this way, one midsummer's day
In a caravan painted all over"
"Which when pig espied, he immediately cried
"Olga Ilena Vladikova"

"Just a wave of her hand in a manner so grand,
"And her caravan rolled down the hill"
"Whereas for pig, he started the jig
Which you see, he is dancing still"

"But she never returned, and poor pig never learned
Of the folly of love at first sight"
"And he dances away not only the day,
But also the whole of the night."

I thanked Mrs Pig for her Trimbledew Pie.
I thanked Mrs Pig for her wine.
I bade her take courage, and try to be brave
As all would come right, given time.

So I said my goodbye and on leaving the sty
Passed poor pig who was still pirouetting.
In spite of the wind, and in spite of the rain,
And was getting a terrible wetting.

I reached the gate, and didn't wait
But started to climb over.
And from the night, I heard pig sigh,
"Sweet Olga Ilena Vladikova"

I once met a pig that was dancing a jig
Right at the top of a hill.
And for all I've heard to the contrary
He is probably dancing there still.

THE EYE

The unseen eye,
The seemingly
Unseeing eye,
…Sees all.

PRAYER

I
Said a prayer,
And
You were there.

IMPRISONED

O sweet and gentle love
Who holds me close to warm and rounded breast?
Imprison me within they self
'Lest foolish-wise I would escape the nest.

Embrace me tight about then,
With limbs that cling like vines,
That I may never leave thee
Or thy love that ever shines.

Make this my eternal sentence
To ever remain here thus,
In thy darkest and sweetest dungeon
Until we are turned to dust.

INVASION

The quiet of the summer evening
Was pierced by the cries
Of a woman being raped,
And, as the wisps of smoke
Drifted about what had once been a village,
Even the setting sun blushed
As it hid its face behind the tops
Of the shivering palm trees.

The flea-bitten dogs of the village,
With singed and still smouldering flesh,
Loped aimlessly from hut to hut
Whimpering and turning now and then
To snap at the cruel invisible fingers
Which, at every step
Prodded deep, and tore
At their pitiful half cooked bodies.

With the coming of the dawn
The jungle slowly came to life
And, to the sound of cockatoo, monkey and giant toad,
The wrinkled old woman
Fanned the dying embers of her home
To boil water in a can, whilst from behind
The lush green curtain of the jungle's edge
Came the soft sound of young girls crying.

A CHANGE OF HEART

"Well that's the end of that" she sighed,
Sitting alone at the bar.
The great romance was officially closed
He'd just driven off in his car.

Three wasted years, with nothing to show,
The way it always ends.
With the usual talk about "right thing to do"
And "hope we can still be friends?"

Right thing to do? Oh yes, for him,
Leaving her in the lurch.
So that he could smile as he walked down the aisle
With his pink cheeked bride in church.

But what had she to look forward to,
Another romance, and then…?
The usual goodbye, in some saloon bar.
Oh God. How she hated men.

With their oily promises to be true
And to love for evermore.
Until a new one catches their eye,
Then you're just another whore.

Then they give you the tale about settling down
With a family of their own,
And you didn't fit in with their plans
And that once again you're alone.

Well, it's not going to happen again, so there,
She promised her mirrored reflection.
And to think, that the only thing she asked
Was a little love and affection.

In the mirror, a face she saw,
A face that was not her own.
With a masculine chin and deep blue eyes,
And those were on her alone.

She turned from the bar, and liked what she saw,
A well cut suit and grey flecked hair.
Then taking a cigarette from her bag
She deliberately threw back the stare.

In a moment the stranger was at her side
And a gold cigarette lighter flickered.
"Allow me" a soft warm voice said.
And somewhere nearby, someone sniggered.

An easy pick-up? ... so what?
She had to have love or die.
Let them think what they like, the bloody fools.
At least it was worth a try.

A moment later, the stranger said,
Staring her straight in the eye.
"I say, it's rather warm in here,
My flat is quite close by"

They walked to the door together,
In a silence almost devout.
And as she stepped through, into the night,
The WOMAN followed her out.

LAMENT TO LOST BEAUTY

See now the wrinkles deeply etched
Where once translucent skin taunt stretched,
Delighted eye of all who saw
And made men burn to see yet more.

And here the hair, once burnished gold,
Now white as snow and just as cold,
Has lost its power to ensnare
Those comely youths to yesteryear.

And gone the form once near divine,
With generous curves and warmth sublime,
That did with all embracing guile,
Cause some to weep, and some to smile.

But now replaced with drooping flesh
Cause no old fires to burn afresh.
And as the time to die draws near,
Lives today, in yesteryear.

DEATH OF A NEW BORN BABE

Yestermorn
A tiny babe was born,
And for a little while
A mother's breast was warm.

What schemes, what dreams
Filled that sweet woman's head.
But when she looked again
Her darling babe was dead.

HUSH SWEET BUTTERCUP

Hush! Sweet buttercup,
Shake not so violent in the breeze
Lest thou should'st wake my own true love
Sleeping cushioned at my knees.

Ring not thy chimes, dear bluebell
Lest thou should'st cause her stir,
And leave undone the golden sleep
My love has brought to her.

Soft, soft fair gentle butterfly
Flap not thy wings so loud.
Take care to not collide I pray
With passing puff of cloud.

Sleep, sleep, my own true love
Whilst I watch over thee,
And so re-dream with open eyes
The pleasure I've shared with thee.

PUBLIC OPINION

Keep your bloody eyes open ref.
Look what he's doing now.
Wanna borrow my glasses?
Watch his fist then --- WOW!

Get round the other side.
There he's done it again.
You couldn't wrestle my mother-in-law.
Oh! The pain, the pain.

Fingers, fingers. Break the hold.
Watch his knee then. Ropes!
Hit him with the soggy end
What a pair of dopes.

What time's the wrestling start then?
Give us our money back.
Laces, laces. Ref wake up,
Time they gave you the sack.

Hit him with your pension book.
Doctor Livingstone --- I presume.
Disqualify him referee.
He wants to leave the room.

Do the same to him then.
Chop him in the belly.
Hurry up and let's get home,
There's wrestling on the telly.

Go on have a go Ma!
Stick your hatpin in him.
You wouldn't come out here then.
That's it, go on chin him.

Hurry up, the pubs'll shut.
You'll miss the last train home.

Pull him by the hair, ref.
Give the dog a bone.
Why don't you learn some new holds?
Warn him for using the chokes.
New holds? You must be kidding!
Why don't YOU learn some new JOKES?

A READY WOMAN

There is no sweetness like the sweetness
Of a ready woman.
No heavy ripening grape
Upon the vine,
Nor luscious bursting
Scarlet fig is so sublime,
As the sweetness of a ready woman.

There is no perfume like the perfume
Of a ready woman.
No Damask Rose
Or hybrid tea,
Nor blossom laden orange tree.
No jasmine, violet or thyme that can compare
With the perfume of a ready woman.

There is no softness like the softness
Of a ready woman.
No bed of feathered down
Whereon to drown
Can bring you soft, perfumed sweetness
Of a ready woman.

IF I HAD THE TIME

If I had the time I'd write a book.
And in the book, I'd take a look
At all the people that I'd met
And even those I hadn't yet.

Those learned scholars of my youth
Those girls who fought with claw and tooth
To gain possession of a Yank
And put his dollars in the bank.

Philosophers and craftsmen too
Who tried to pass on what they knew.
Villains, heroes, tough guys, wimps,
Wide eyed Botticelli imps.

Memories of friends that died
Cold nights on a mountainside.
Creamy skinned girls with silken hair
Torturous, evil, dentist's chair.

Tales I would tell of nights spent in Hell
Of the numerous battles I'd won.
Of a stolen kiss from an innocent Miss
And long lazy days in the sun.

Villains and heroes, and modern day Neros
Would cram every line on the page.
Wisdom and wit would both play their bit
And earn me the title of 'Sage'.

My friends would surround me and laud me
My enemies flee in dismay.
For fear of my pen I'd be feted
For my favours, the whole world would pay.

Such then are the things I would publish
For the wide, wide world to read,

My pen would be rapier
To aid the millions in need.
My name would become immortal
They'd build me a white marble tomb
And pilgrims would take their hats off
As they showed them into my room.

If I had the time I'd write a book
With wisdom on every line.
But I fear this will never come to pass
For I just haven't got the time.

REINCARNATION

I was a man
Lost in a beautiful valley.
The air was warm and scented.
Ahead were two twin peaks
Thrusting their pink tips into the sky.

Behind me was the dark secret forest.

I was a flea
Lost in the navel of a beautiful woman.
The air was warm and scented.
Ahead were two twin peaks
Thrusting their pink tips into the sky.

Behind me was the dark secret forest.

VOICES

Voice of the white man.

    Kick them all out
    The dirty bastards.
    Kick them all back
    To their own country.

    Coming here, taking our women
    And taking the bread from the mouths of our children.

    This land belongs to us.
    They hate us, and we hate them
    So kick them all out.
    Kick them all back
    To their own country.

Voice of the black man

    Kick them all out,
    The dirty bastards.
    Kick them all back
    To their own country.

    Coming here, taking our women
    And taking the bread from the mouths of our children.

    This land belongs to us.
    They hate us, and we hate them
    So kick them all out.
    Kick them all back
    To their own country.

Voice from the grave

Listen to the noisy ignorant bastards
Making all that noise up there.

Coming here and walking all over us.
Black and white. White and black.
Don't they know this land belongs to us?
And that in a hundred years
We'll all be the same colour?

Kick them all out.
Kick them all back
To their own country.

AFTERMATH

Fused into the oneness
By the very sweat,
That marks the labour
Of our love,
All passion spent, we hesitate,
Whilst darkness presses from above.
For in this moment in between,
First the ecstasy, then the void,
We try recapturing in vain,
The appetites so deeply cloyed.

36 BUS

Just before nine, there's a bus comes along
That takes you to Camberwell Green.
There's pushing and shoving and "After you love", 'ing
And old hysterical scene.

A mum gets pushed by some callous youth
With lank and long greasy hair
Whose aim is to follow that short skirt upstairs
With a fixed and hungry stare.

And there's men with coughs and city toffs
And some with pipes that don't light.
And ladies with knitting, and some just sitting,
And some re-dreaming last night.

Young girls with giggles, and soft sexy wiggles.
Eavesdropping pimply faced boys.
With hands in their pockets and eyes straining sockets,
They anticipate marital joys.

The Daily Mirror, The Times, The Sun,
The Mail, The Daily Express.
A glimpse of thigh from a skirt too high,
A straining and crumpled dress.

Hair combed across shining baldpate
Like the lines in an exercise book.
Midnight blue mohair white collar and cuffs.
A Parson, a Wage-Clerk, a Crook.

Reds, Blues and Greens, Tee-shirts and jeans,
Turtle-necked jerseys and belts.
Leaky umbrellas, smart coloured fellahs,
Suede shoes, worn down to the welts.

Loud screaming babes, skins of all shades
Clutching at jam covered toys.
Old ladies fainting "is'ing and aint'ing"
Blaming it all on the noise.

Ding on the bell. "You go to Hell"
"I gave you two and six"
"Terrible headache" "Excuse me please"
"She's in a terrible fix"

Apprentices joking sixth-formers smoking,
Schoolgirls with mascara'ed eyes.
"Sorry, full up, one right behind"
Fat man with unbuttoned flies.

Buxom wench, terrible stench.
"Open your window please"
"Standing room only" "This shilling's phoney"
"Not if he went on his knees"

Varicose veins, pregnancy pains.
Imitation fur coat.
Dandruff on jacket. "He's worth a packet"
"Sit down you're rocking the boat"

"Been queuing up since half-past eight,
Aint this bleeding bus slow!"
"CAMBERWELL GREEN... All off you lot"
"This is as far as we go"

WOMAN

Look well to it
That never in thy wildest ecstasy
Should'st though blind thine eyes
With that which pleases most.

Remember well, her name is Woman,
And she, is ever ready with twining arms and legs
To trap thee
And hold thee captive 'till the end of time.

Be on guard against her softness,
For it is the softness of the swamp,
That will quickly and quietly
Engulf thee.

Be on guard against her tears
Lest they
Should'st wear away
Thine heart of stone.

Fall not prey to her perfume
For it is with this
She will intoxicate and ensnare thee
For ever.

Thus then… is Woman,
Who thou should take care to love
With open eyes,
Or… love not at all.

THE LITTLE BOY SAID

"Me Da's run away"
The little boy said.
"He's left me and me Mam
And me sister."
And then in a whisper
"Mister" he said,
"For all that we know
He may even be dead"

THE UGLY GIRL

These pink rimmed eyes that squint and stare,
This crooked nose and matted hair,
These ears too large, and heavy chin,
This mouth too wide, and lips too thin,
Will prompt no love in any man
And speaks untruths of what I am.

For, within this clumsy frame
Burns love as fierce as any flame.
But I shall never catch his eye
And there's little I can do, but sigh.
He only sees the things men wish to see,
And thus my hidden virtues to him remain a mystery.

BLISS

Was there ever such bliss
Like stealing a kiss
From a lovely young Miss
On a night such as this?

AMID THE NEW MOWN HAY

Soft and sweet were the games we played
Amid the new mown hay.

Yet softer still was the love we made
At the end of a perfect day.

And just as we, that day did help
To reap the harvest, earlier sown.

So did we, in time ourselves
Gather a harvest of our own.

DRESSING ROOM

Part One.

See that bloke in the corner,
Putting on his shoes?
Should have packed up years ago,
All he does, is lose.

Make way for chaps like me
What's got a bit of fire.
Underneath my name they print
"Never known to tire."

I'll get to the top, I will.
No-one will stand in my way.
I'll break their bodies, and break their hearts
If that's the only way.

Not for me, the crummy pre-lims
And a bus-ride home in the dark.
I'll make myself a packet
And have myself a lark.

Part Two

(Same dressing room, same man, but several years later)

That flash young bastard over there
With his velvet dressing gown.
Calls himself a wrestler,
More like a bleeding clown.

Like to meet him in the ring
Just for a round or two.
I'd give him "The Blond Adonis"
I'd kick him black and blue.

Fancy putting him top of the bill
And a bloke like me at the bottom.
How'd they expect you to give your best
When you feel so bloody rotten?

If I'd stayed at the top a year or two more
Things wouldn't have been so bad.
But it's having it rubbed in by the kids like him
That makes me feel so mad.

PATTERNS IN THE DUST

In this vast eternal plan
We are, but shapes
That move about the earth
Leaving our tiny patterns in the dust.
Knowing full well that all our little ills
Are but the newly ripened fruits
Of yesterday's unbridled lust.

TEMPTATION

To all intents and purposes
There's few men can resist,
The softness of a woman's lips
Just asking to be kissed.

And even those who say they can,
Just given half a chance,
Will leave the straight and narrow path
And lead a merry dance.

And thus it ever has been
And thus it ever will,
For nature gave us appetites,
That need must have their fill.

ODE TO A NOCTURNAL CREATURE

What are you doing,
... little one?
Why hide your face
From the morning sun?

Why not sleep at night
And work by day,
And in between...
Find time to play?

GRAVESIDE

By an open grave one day
I sat me down to think.
Of this and that and other things
Of he that lay beyond the brink.

John Brown, his name, I knew him well.
A person of some note.
A Magistrate, an M.P. too,
In fact he'd got my vote.

A self-made man, he'd often said,
And well I do believe,
And yet, somehow I find it strange
That I alone am here to grieve.

His house was always full,
His chosen company, most gay.
But now the hour has come to say 'Adieu',
I alone have seen him on his way.

Cold blows the wind, dark grows the sky
Duty done, I must away.
Cold grows the ground, bats flutter by,
Be this the hour when night meets day?

EPITAPH

Stay a while, and spare a smile
For he who is buried here.
And do not weep or feel sorry,
Remember your time is near.

And bear on this, he has found such bliss
That in life he was not able.
And lays here sleeping in the warmth
Of Mother Nature's cradle.

EPITAPH FOR A GLOBE-TROTTING WRESTLER

Sleep now the gentle sleep
For thy last bout is won,
And this, thy last reward,
To lay here sleeping in the sun.

Dream now the dreams undreamt,
Wait not upon the morrow.
For thee, all time does now combine
To keep without, all sorrow.

Rest now thy fever'd brain which on this earth,
So filled itself with larger dreams of life.
And at the end betrayed thee and led thee here to die
Unmourned by any wife.

CAN THIS BE LOVE?

Can this be love? Then give me more,
For this is all I ask.
And if perchance there is no more,
Then make this breath my last.

THE ADDICT

Now the gentle honey fills my vein.
How sweet it is,
Absorbing all the pain.

Now lifts the veil from o'er my heavy eyes.
How beautiful
The fields of Paradise.

Now starts the dream, the mystic lands, the moon.
Now fades the dream,
So soon? So soon?

How dark it is, now starts the other dreams.
The voices, faces, shapes,
The moans, and then… the screams.

In the darkness now I hear them stir.
Will they come again tonight?

Tonight I think they'll come again
And walk about my wall.
And some of them are tiny,
And some of them are tall.
And some of them wear top hats,
And some of them have horns,
And some of them wear yellow spats,
And some of them have corns.
And some of them, they hate me.
And some of them are blue,
And some of them are old,
And some of them are new.
And some of them are singing,
And some of them are dumb,
And some of them have fingers,
And some of them have none.
And some of them are real
And some of them are dreams.
And some of them are touching me,
My hands, my face, my… (he screams).

THE WEDDING

They stood together
Huddled there, swaying
Like a giant rhododendron bush
In full bloom.

"Let me in" screamed the fat lady,
"Let me in, I'm the bride's mother."
Like some poor lost soul
Screaming outside the gates of Heaven.

Friends of the family.
Armed with brownies and instamatics,
They fidget and jostle, taking their headless photos
To hand down to posterity.

Tiny-tot bridesmaids, like little Christmas tree fairies,
Savagely jerked into position by proud mums,
To face the click, click, clicking
Of the hungry cannibal cameras.

Smug bride.
Dressed in virgin white of course.
Trying hard to fill the role,
Pretending she doesn't know we know.

Bridegroom! Fish on a hook!
Man the hunter? Poor fish.
Captured, tried and sentenced
Within the space of a few minutes.

More poses by the car for the click clickers.
Maternal tears, and away.
He thinks not of reception laid ahead,
His thoughts go further still, to hungry waiting cannibal bed

THE TRAMP

Trickle, trickle, splish, splash, splosh.
Down the neck of my mackintosh,
Comes the ever incessant rain
Monotonously driving me insane.

Squish, squash, squelch, go my shoes,
Little wonder I've got the blues.
Surely there's more to life than this,
Waiting and praying for death's final kiss?

Somewhere the sun is shining bright.
Somewhere the stars are twinkling at night.
Somewhere a body is cosy and warm.
Somewhere they're happy to see the dawn.

But me, I wander deserted street
Averting the gaze of all I meet.
For I'm an outcast, a dirty tramp
Who isn't supposed to feel the damp.

But better days I swear I've seen,
And it's tragic to think, after what I've been,
That I have to end up in this dismal way
Tramping the streets by night and day.

But I've had my chance and let it slip,
And now for the price of a good night's kip,
My soul, to the Devil himself, I'd sell,
And spend my eternity burning in Hell.

SALES TALK

Order early for Christmas.
Only a few more left.
Free gifts with every purchase.
The wages of sin is death.

Do-it-yourself and save money.
This amazing toy can be yours.
By order of the executors.
Small deposit secures.

Saves you time and money.
Can be used by a child.
No more sooty chimneys.
Fourteen days free trial.

Special New Year offer.
Costs a penny a week to run.
You can be your own boss.
Holidays in the sun.

I was a skinny weakling.
Be cremated by post.
Develop a 99" bust.
Be the girl with the most.

A genuine sacrifice… must sell.
A thousand pounds to be won.
Owner going abroad.
Two for the price of one.

Help the poor and needy.
Learn karate, and kill.
Every method fully explained.
Including of course the pill.

Make your neighbours envy you.
Eggs from free-range chickens.
Plots for sale in the Bahamas.
Complete set of Charles Dickens

Interflora. Intercham.
Now showing at the Troxy.
Prove to her you love her.
Intercourse, by Proxy.

HYPOCRITES

How brave we are, how wise, how good,
We lead our lives the way we should.
We bend our knees on the seventh day,
And raise our eyes to God and pray.

Knowing full well that we alone
Need never for our sins atone.
For we are blameless of all guilt
And innocent of all blood spilt.

So we alone deserve the prize,
To gaze on God with honest eyes,
And whilst 'you' burn for eternity,
So 'we', shall live in majesty.

THE FAILURE

Despondent I, can only sit and sigh.
Reviewing long lost chances,
Inviting curious glances
As I dribble in my glass and wipe a rheumy eye.

Once I was an upright lad,
Bold and straight and true.
But bit by bit, I descended the pit
And the warnings all came true.

And now there is little left to say,
Except that I wait for the final day
When all will come right, and all will come well,
And I am allotted my place… in HELL.

THE PRICE OF FRIENDSHIP

To think, to think, our friendship ends
For the sake of so few dollars
And yet we men of pen and ink
Are not such learned scholars.

That we must turn the other cheek
To take fresh blows anew
When after all, we only ask
For that which is our due.

And so, dear friend, I beg you pause
And think on that which gives me cause
To ruminate thus, in this vein
Your chance to make amends may never come again!

LONG, LONG AGO

I remember
The tramlines
That twisted
Through my distant youth
And held together
My age of innocence.
I remember
When for a penny
I could bare my body to the sun
And leap from high
Into a seething mass
Of unwashed, shrieking and screaming humanity,
That twisted
And jerked spasmodically,
Churning the cloudy chlorine swelling water to foam,
And with rigid skinny arms,
Splashed all
Who came within their reach.

I remember
When a sixpenny all day ticket
Was my passport
To board the iron monster
And be carried
To far flung places.
To Eltham, Southend Pond
And Abbey Wood.
To Battersea Park and Clapham Common.
We'd clank our way
With metal studded boots
Up the iron stairs
To commandeer the huge round seat
Above the driver's head
And help to steer
Our ship
Through the bustling sunny streets.
For in those days… it was always sunny.

TOO LATE

I met an old friend yesterday
As he upon his death-bed lay,
And knowing not his time was near
He told me his plans for the coming year.

"I've always worked too hard" he said
"And so I've ended up in bed,
But when they let me out of here
I'll make up for it, never fear."

Now there is a moral to learn from this,
That whilst our life is not all bliss
We shouldn't wait until the end
Or we'll all end up like my dear old friend.

THE FOUR AGES OF MAN

I have eaten liquorice
And dare not laugh or smile.
If Mamma saw my black, black teeth
She'd chase me for a while.

I have been into the barn
With pretty Mary Lou,
And there would be the Hell to pay
If her big brother knew.

I have tasted bitter words,
As sharp as any knife,
For I no longer live alone
But have a loving wife.

They've given me the sacrament
Because my time is near
And 'though the birds will greet the dawn,
Their song I'll never hear.

THE KNELL

Ding, dong, the bell.
Whose knell, whose knell
That sounds on yonder hill?

Not mine, not mine
I'm pleased to say,
For I am with thee still.

EMBAKMENT GARDENS

We sat in the park that afternoon.
We sat in the park and didn't feel the cold.
That wooden bench was our island
Where we crossed legs, fidgeted and talked and talked.

Three times I asked if you were cold
Three times you answered "no" and let me feel your hand.
I found it warm, as warm as mine
And yet, we both were trembling.

William Tyndall gave me a bronze scowl from his stone pedestal
To mark his disapproval of what we were about, but we didn't care.
Afterwards when we walked up Villiers Street, towards the Strand
The bookshops winked at us.

There were couples everywhere
Couples walking with their heads close together
And it wasn't until then that I realised
I hadn't even kissed you.

ON THE ROOF

It's nice to sit in the shadows
With my feet sticking out in the sun.
And look up the hill at the olive groves
That have given me so much fun.

If I turn my head at an angle
Of forty-five degrees,
I can see the top of the waterfall
Nestling among the trees.

At the side of that, there's the castle
That dominates the town.
Wearing her battered tiara
Like Queen Victoria's crown.

And the faded pink of the rooftops
On every side I can see.
And that wrinkled old man across the street
Who whistles and waves to me.

And the white of the new apartments
That climb higher every year.
And the midnight blue of the mountains
That appear deceivingly near.

And in the smoke of the charcoal burners
Working high on the mountainside.
Gradually scraping the surface bare,
As sure as an incoming tide.

And the blue, blue sky all around,
And the shadows growing longer.
And the braying of the distant ass,
As his working days get longer.

The raucous voice on the radio
That tells us to "Cha-cha-cha"
The tooting of ever impatient horn,
That signals each passing car.

I can see it all from the rooftop
As I lay in the sun getting brown.
And there's nowhere on earth I would rather be,
Than this lovely, sleepy town.

FUNERAL MARCH

It's a winding road that leads up the hill
To where the green cypresses stand.
And I've travelled it many times in my mind,
In time to the village band.

And wherever I've been, and whatever I've seen,
At the end of each busy day,
I sit for a while, and I have to smile,
Perhaps that's the way I pray.

For where else on earth is the grass so sweet
Or the trees so straight and true,
As that place on the hill overlooking the town
'Neath a sky of azure blue?

So don't be sad for your poor old dad
If you have to follow his pall,
Just keep in step with the fellow in front
And the crash of the waterfall.

And remember that's where I want to sleep,
Right at the top of the hill
To keep an eye on the Liri
And the old ruined paper mill

THE BELL OF SAN LORENZO

The bell in yonder steeple chimes the hour
And in a short time yet, will sound again.
Oblivious to all, it has the power
To conquer time, impervious to sun and rain.

And 'ere that promised hour has been, and passed,
And just as certain as the sun will greet the coming morn.
Somewhere in this world a life will end,
And somewhere else a new babe born.

For such it ever was decreed,
That nature with her magic wand,
Would reap the harvest, sow the seed,
And thus perpetuate the bond.

For he who made the universe,
With clear far-seeing eye,
Wrote by our names in his little book
The moment when each should die.

And who then are we to say that we'll hear
The pealing of bell when next it sounds,
Or with any certainty be here,
Instead of sleeping 'neath our grassy mounds?

Think well then, on these simple words.
Appreciate the flowers and birds.
For nature's appetite must be fed.
Remember you're a long time dead.

DEATH OF A CAESAR, 1970

"The pen is mightier than the sword"
The journalists said
And, as if to prove it,
They stabbed him to death
With their ball-point pens.

WINTER

See how the wind
Picks the leaves
From the shivering
Willow tree,
And plucks at the thatch
Of the shepherd's sleepy hut
Seeking futile shelter
On the leeside
Of the hill
As the earth snuggles warm
Under it's blanket of snow,
Leaving us
Out in the cold.

RESOLUTION

As we near
The end of the journey, of that
Which some call life,
It would be as well
If we thought awhile
On the things
That have caused us strife.

Of the major and minor incidents
We've encountered along the way.
That somehow are not so important now
As they seemed in a bygone day.

And by doing so,
To resolve ourselves
That the end
Is drawing nigh,
And then to make up
For the time we've lost,
And to live life… before we die.

THE MAN WHO NEVER WOULD

There was a man who never would
Take his place in queues,
But leaned against the traffic lights
And read the morning news.

Then, when the bus slowed down,
Or sometimes had to stop,
He would fold his paper neatly
And on the bus he'd hop.

This was his game for many years
Until the fatal day
When just about to hop aboard
The driver pulled away.

Instead of landing on the bus
He landed in the road
Whilst just behind another bus
Came speeding with its load.

The council sent three men with brooms
And one to lend a hand.
And when they'd tidied up the spot
They sprinkled it with sand.

The moral of this little tale
Should not be hard to find
Never, never, hop a bus,
There's always one behind.

THE PRISONER

Mark well how the poison works!
See, his eyes begin to cloud.
Watch then his fingers clutch
Like talons 'bout his burning throat.

Note how he staggers back and forth
As the dungeon walls
Close in about his head,
See the frothing at the lips.

The blanching skin now turns to purple hue,
His twitching form spreadeagle's on the floor.
In vain the wordless curses pass our heads,
Dead, dead, dead… he'll trouble us no more.

ANOTHER DAY

There isn't much to say.
Today's another day,
And yesterday has gone forever.

Tomorrow, when it comes will bring its share of sorrows,
And all our yesterdays will merge
………. with our tomorrows.

THE STRANGE BIRD

There lives at the base of the Liggymoo Tree
A most amazing bird,
For though he sings to his love all day
His notes just can not be heard.

And soft is his song, and twice as long
As his cousin's the Tingalingoose.
He wears top hats and yellow spats
And has laces in both of his shoes.

He starts the day in the usual way
By pursuing the Financial Times
But long before breakfast is over
He is busy composing new rhymes.

And it's rumoured he's soon to be married
To a parrot named Jessica Rose,
Who has silken red and blue feathers
And a wart on the end of her nose.

And I'm sure they will be very happy
In the house on the Pennine Chains,
For the only time they'll go out for a walk
Is the morning after it rains.

THE SAILOR'S LAMENT

There came three men one winter's eve
Their hair was white as snow.
They bade me hurry to take leave
For a journey we must go.

"Yes a journey we must go" they said
"To the land of no return"
"To the twilight land of the living dead,
Where the fierce, bright fires burn."

I tried in vain, to call the name
Of my true love far away
To tell her of the white haired men
And the awful game they play.

To bid her not to wait for me
Or to set the wedding day
For I saw by the look in their cold grey eyes
That I'd never get away.

So somewhere now she waits for me
At the edge of the silvery sands
And cries for her poor lost sailor boy,
Who sailed to foreign lands.

And the three gaunt men with snow white hair
Still travel far and wide
And my own true love still weeps for me
Down at the edge of the tide.

But never more will I see her face
Or kiss her soft brown hair,
For the twilight land of the living dead
Is not for her to share.

So all you sailor boys beware
If ever you should see,
The three gaunt men with snow white hair
As you sail upon the sea.

And if you have a true love fair
Then best stay by her side.
Or she will stand and weep for you
At the edge of the hungry tide.

AD INFINITUM

If we could but see ourselves
With our children's eyes,
We would see reflected in ourselves
The image of our own fathers.
Then perhaps we might begin
To understand the secret of life.

For we would see that we are but custodians
Of that which has gone before,
And guardians of that
Which is yet to come.
For be assured, that in each and every one of us
There is part of someone else.

And if only for this reason,
We should at all times
Be kind and tolerant to others.
For in hurting them
We may well be
Hurting ourselves.

A L O N E

Thou art dead my lonely one
And I am left alone,
And never more will I laugh and sing
For my very soul has flown.

FRED

An old mate of mine whose name was Fred
Awoke one morn to find he was dead.
And not knowing quite how to take the news
He got out of bed, and put on his shoes.

Then seeing his poor self lying there
He put on his trousers and pulled up a chair.
And looking back on the life he had led
He thought to himself "I'm better off dead."

For Fred had been a bit of a lad,
In fact there were some who would say he'd been bad.
And it grieved him to think of it ending this way
Without being given a moment to pray.

There were many things he repented he'd done
And saw all too late the true cost of his fun.
So filled with remorse and shame, was poor Fred,
That he took off his shoes, and went back to bed.

SWEET AND GENTLE MISTRESS MINE

O' sweet and gentle mistress mine
With lips as red as ruby wine.
Turn thy soft brown eyes my way,
And so begin our perfect day.

For waiting on your morning smile,
The day has not begun.
Until I glimpse thy pearly teeth
There is no morning sun.

CHILDREN PLAYING

Happy little children, playing in the sunshine.
How I envy you your lot, wish that it were mine.

Stamping tiny footprints in the heavy dust.
Building, breaking, mending, as all children must.

Not for you the care and worry of a world gone mad.
Today is yours to play and sing, so why should you be sad?

But lo' the sun creeps westward and the shadows falling,
Wrap their mantle round you, mother night is calling.

Soon you'll be in dreamland, dressed in shining armour.
Winning all your battles, knighted for your valour.

Now the day is ended and you're fast asleep.
It's for us, the grown-up ones, to lay awake and weep.

WHEN I WAS LITTLE

When I was little it never rained,
And the sun, it always shone.
But now I am old and feel the cold
Those summer days are gone.

When I was little, I loved the world,
And thought the world loved me.
But now I am old, I know too well
Such things can never be.

When I was little, I used to cry,
For the days when I'd be a man.
But now I am old, I sit and sigh
When I think of what I am.

INCOME TAX

Insidious, creeping, Income Tax.
Confronting us with forms and facts.
Assessments under Schedule D's,
Slowly brings us to our knees.

This was no part of God's vast plan,
To subjugate and humble, man.
Whom he made to walk the earth
Proud and upright from his birth.

This is all a cunning plot,
To bleed us dry, so we have not
The will or power to resist
And then they'll cross us off their list.

When we, like robots live and move,
Only in allotted groove,
Then alone they will emerge,
The fiends behind this evil purge.

And we the subjugated mass
Will slave to keep these tyrants, crass,
So rise up now, cast off your chain.
Your chance may never come again.

SPACE

How vast the sky
And all those twinkling stars
How very far away.
And yet, and yet I feel
That they are part of me.
And when they shine
They shine for me.
And when they seem
As if they are not there,
It is because they close their eyes
To weep for all the loneliness we share.

CUPID

Cupid came on hurried wings
One lovely summer day
And settled for a little while
To watch two children play.

Deep in their unsuspecting hearts
He placed two tiny seeds,
And hid them well that in the years
They'd meet each other's needs.

And though they both trod different paths
That twisted through the following years,
In time those paths did cross again
And cause them shed such joyous tears.

And so it was that in the end
They each became, more than a friend,
And Cupid smiled down from above
To see the ripening of their love.

TEASE

Why I tease you
I do not know.

But I do dear
And so…

For all the times
I've made you cry,

Forgive me,
And your sweet eyes dry.

THE PLEASURE AND THE PROFIT

Such sweetness was not meant for me
And yet it's come my way.
And so I fain must profit
And harvest every day.

For this I know, that life is short
And soon I will be done,
So while I'm here, I'll make good cheer
Until my time has run.

So when I then pass over,
At least I will have known,
The pleasure and the profit,
Of all the seed I've sown.

PROMISES

When they bury my body beneath the ground
At the place at the top of the hill.
Then will I love thee still my love,
Then will I love thee still.

When from my heart a Cypress grows
Pointing straight up to the skies,
Then will I love thee true my love,
As true as the light in thine eyes.

When even my dust, has turned to dust,
Long after my body grows cold,
Then will I love thee still my love.
Just as I did of old.

ONE MOVEMENT

Our journey through the endless space
Weaves the step with delicate ease
Like fine lace,
With dextrous hands
Intermingling through the web of time.
One movement.

Do not move even for a moment
Let's linger in the lanes.
Oh the pain, the pleasures, the pain.
One movement
Too exquisite to explain.

E G O

Give me a pint in a tankard,
No, make it a gin and lime.
No sense in straining the bladder,
So near to closing time.

That's my reflection in the mirror
Not bad for pushing fifty.
Tweed sports coat and yellow check shirt,
Must say I look pretty nifty.

Like to keep myself fit you know,
With a round of golf or two.
Quite a ladies man they say,
And I must admit it's true.

See that young bird in the corner?
Been giving me the eye all night.
Think I'll go and chat her up,
Figure she must be half tight.

Saunter, suave and nonchalant,
Cigarette dangling and chuffed.
"Haven't we met before my dear?"
…"Do me a favour… Get stuffed!"

TO A YOUNG MAIDEN

(Spoken in a garden)

Sweet rosebud, just about to open.
As yet the colour has not touched your cheek
But in a short while now
You will bloom in all your glory.

Then, you will be the Queen,
And all that gaze upon you
Will hold their breath
In wonderment.

And breathing
Your perfumed halo
They will say,
"She indeed is Queen"

But only for a little while, for other rosebuds blooming fresh
Will catch their fickle eye.
The rosy blush will leave your cheek,
And then alas, you'll die.

SEA GRAVE

At the bottom of the sea
There's a graveyard
Of white and hollow bones
And there the sea anemones
And starfish make their homes.

And the move of the tide
From far and wide
Brings flowers and gifts of gold,
Which it heaps on the bones of the dead ones
To stop them from growing cold.

THE LOST PLAYMATE

Two little boys walked on the beach
And threw stones into the sea.
And one of the little boys was you
And the other was me.

Oh what happy hours we spent
Down on the edge of the tide.
And oh what jolly games we played.
Then suddenly, you died.

Now one little boy, walks on the beach
And throws stones into the sea.
Dreaming of days that can never return,
And that little boy is me.

WHEN I'M NOT THERE

What do you do
When I'm not there ?

As you look in the mirror
To comb your hair,
Do you say to yourself
"I wonder if he,
At this very moment
Is thinking of me?"

What do you do
When I'm not there?

When it's time to sleep
Do you say a prayer,
Then sigh to your pillow
The words we must hide
And pretend that it's me
Laying there by your side?

WHY PICK ON ME?

Why pick on me…?
I mean to say…
From all the fellows
That came your way.
There must have been one
I do suppose
That didn't have
A broken nose.
Or shuffle his feet
Or look at the ground
When other people
Are standing around.
Don't you think
You could have done better
Instead of a sermon
With every letter?
He'd no doubt have sent you
Gifts of gold
And probably wouldn't have been
Half as old
As this writer of verse
Whose manner is terse
And whose mode of life
Is probably worse
Than any other
You could have had,
And who's old enough to be
… Your Dad?

THE FLAME

The flame
So clean, so bright.
The flame
Challenging the night.

Pointing
Like a finger to the sky
Where
The heavy storm clouds thunder by.

Fighting for its life
Against the wind.
Crooks its finger
Beckoning.

"Hold on, I come
To save you from the fate"
"Hold on" I cry,
But know it is too late.

The flame
So clean, so bright.
Has vanished
In the night.

IN CONCLUSION

… And thus do we all, each of us
Have influence upon the life of others.

For opinions that we now voice, may well in time
Send waves of sound however faint

To touch upon some ultra sensitive ear, and in so doing
Start a train of thought that will feed an appetite,

Or fan an all consuming fire of hate,
Or plant a tiny seed of love.

So should we, then, at all times
Be most careful in our thoughts.

Paying even more care to utterances,
For it is these, if ill judged,

Can cause most harm
To all about us

Not least of all
Unto ourselves.

ME

I'm a wrestling referee
Who happens to write poetry,
And should you like my little book
Now that you've taken time to look,
I'll be as happy as can be
And that's reward enough for me.

THE END

…And so we reach
The final page.
Wrinkled now
And yellowed with age.
And as we take
Our last long look,
Suddenly…
Snaps shut… the book.